From Branson With LOL Pocket Edition

Christopher James

Branson, Missouri, USA

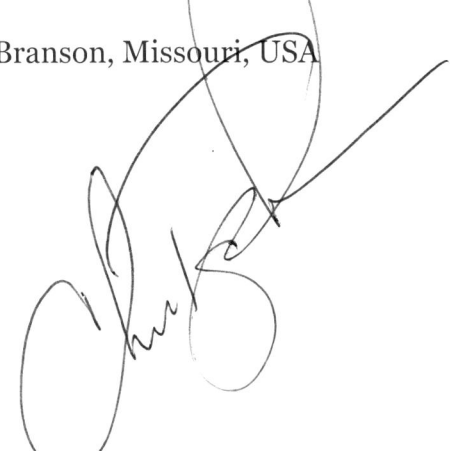

From Branson with LOL: Pocket Edition

Copyright © 2014 by Christopher James

All rights reserved. No part of this publication may be reproduced, stored in a retrieval system, or transmitted by any means – electronic, mechanical, photographic (photocopying), recording, or otherwise – without prior permission in writing from the author.

Printed in the United States of America

ISBN: 978-0-9855789-3-0

Learn more information at: funnyhypermagicboy.com

Dedicated to my wife, Rachael, our twins, Alexander and Cassandra, and the one girl that can always make me laugh and smile, Olivia Vanessa

There is never a shortage of material as a professional comedian. I find humor in every day life and situations, sometimes to the dismay of those around me. It's a gift and a curse. Over the years, I have found a career in comedy to not only be theraputic, but also very rewarding. People are never shy about sharing a joke or a funny anecdote after a show. One thing I have learned, everyone loves to laugh.

Anyone that has ever seen my show, knows that I like to have something for everyone. I include jokes for every age, lifestyle, and intellectual level. I like to include simple puns and annecdotes and few jokes that will make the audience think.

This book is a compilation of many things. First, it's jokes, stories and annecdotes I've collected over the years from audience members and friends.

Second, it's my own style of humor and jokes from my show and personal life. Third, there are some jokes that I have purchased from professionals over the years. And last, it's some of the stories and jokes that have been passed down from generation to generation. Some oldies but goodies that still bring a smile, no matter how corny.

    I've organized this book in the style of my own show. A mixture that will leave you thinking one minute, groaning the next, and laughing a paragraph later. Not every joke is for everyone. However, I feel there is something for everyone.

    Enjoy.

A man dies and appears at the Pearly Gates. "Have you ever done a good deed?" asks St. Peter.

"Sure, one time I came across a gang of bikers who were threatening a woman," the man says. "I walked up to the leader and punched him the face, kicked over his bike, and told him, " You leave her alone, or you'll answer to me."

"That was very brave of you," says St. Peter. "When did this happen?"

"About five minutes ago."

A blonde who's having financial troubles decides to kidnap a child for ransom. She writes on a piece of paper: "I've kidnapped your son. Leave $10,000 behind the oak tree in the park tomorrow at 7 AM. The blonde." She walks over to the park, grabs a little boy, pins the note to his jacket and tells him to run home.

The next morning, the blonde goes back to the park, where she sees the boy standing behind the oak tree.

"I'm supposed to give you this," he says, handing her a brown bag. As she counts the money, she notices a new note pinned to his jacket: "For the records, I can't believe that one blonde would do this to another."

A man is feeling depressed and decides to see a psychiatrist. He gets to the office, lies down on the couch, and tells the doctor his life story.

"I know exactly what your problem is," says the psychiatrist. "It's a simple matter of low self-esteem."

"Oh," says the man, dejected.

"Don't worry," says the doctor. "It's very common among losers like you."

An elderly man lying on his deathbed catches a whiff of homemade chocolate chip cookies wafting up the stairs. He gathers his strength and makes his way down to the kitchen. Just as he's reaching for the plate of cookies, his wife suddenly smacks him on the hand with a wooden spoon.

"Stay out of those," she yells. "They're for the funeral!"

On his first day at a new job, a guy attempts to phone an intern. "Bring me a cup of coffee pronto," he bellows.

"Do you know who you're talking to?" the voice on the other end of the line shouts back. "This is the president of the company!"

"Do you know who YOU are taking to, buddy?" the guy yells.

"No, I don't," replies the president.

"Thank goodness for that!"

"I've found a great job," a man says to his wife. "A 10 AM start, a 6 PM finish, no overtime, no weekends, and it pays $2,000 a week in cash."

"That's unbelievable," says the wife.

"I know, "says the husband. "You start Monday."

A man approaches a beautiful woman in a supermarket.

"I've lost my girlfriend," he tells her. "Can you stand here and talk to me for a few minutes?"

"Sure, but I don't understand how that would help," she replies.

"Well, every time I talk to a beautiful woman like you, my girlfriend appears out of nowhere."

Doctors say I have a multiple personality, but we don't agree with that.

"I have some good news and I have some bad news," says the doctor.

"OK," says the patient. "Give me the good news first."

"Well," says the doctor, "they're going to name a disease after you…"

A redneck is walking down the road one day when he sees his cousin coming toward him carrying a gunnysack.

"Hey there, Billy Ray," says the redneck. "Whatcha got?"

"Some chickens," replies the cousin.

"If I kin guess how many you got, kin I have one?"

"Shoot, if you guess right, I'll give you both of 'em."

"OK...Five."

Little Amy is in her backyard filling a big hole with dirt, occasionally smacking it down with her shovel. Her curious neighbor peers over the fence. "What are you doing there, Amy?" he asks.

"I'm...I'm burying my goldfish," she replies tearfully.

"Oh, sorry," he says, "but isn't that an awfully big hole for a goldfish?"

Amy pats down the last heap of earth, looks up, and says, "That's because he's inside your stupid cat!"

"I knew I had a problem with dyslexia the day I went to a toga party dressed as a goat."

A Frenchman with a parrot perched on his shoulder walks into a bar. The bartender says, "Wow, that's really neat! Where did you get him?"

"In France," the parrot replies. "They've got millions of 'em."

A burglar breaks into a house one night and turn on his flashlight to find an expensive stereo. As he approaches it, a voice behind him whispers, "Jesus is watching you."

The startled burglar turns and shines his light on a caged parrot in the corner of the room.

"Was that you?" asks the burglar.

"Yes," answers the parrot. "My name is Moses. How do you do? Squawk!"

Amused at the talking bird, the burglar laughingly asks, "What kind of people name a parrot Moses?"

"Squawk! The same kind of people who name a Rottweiler Jesus."

Dear Son:

I'm writing this slow cause I know you can't read fast.

We don't live where we did when you left. Your Dad read in the paper where most accidents happen within twenty miles of the house, so we moved. This place has a washing machine. The first day I put four shirts in it, pulled the chain, and haven't seen them since.

It's only rained twice this week. Three days the first time and four days the second time.

The coat you wanted me to send, your Aunt Sue said was too heavy to mail with all those big buttons on it so we cut them off and they're in the pockets.

We got a bill from the funeral home, said if we didn't make the last payment on Grandma's funeral, up she comes.

Your Uncle Joe fell in the whisky vat yesterday -- some men tried to pull him out but he fought 'em all off and finally drowned. We cremated him right after and he's still burning good this morning.

Three of your friends went off the bridge in a pick-up truck, one was driving, two in the back. The driver rolled the window down and swam out. The two in the back couldn't get the tailgate open so they drowned too.

Not much news this time, nothing much happens round here, will try to write more next time.

Love, Your Mama

P.S. Was gonna send you some money but already had this sealed up.

A blonde goes into the doctor's office and says that her body hurts wherever she touches it.

"That's odd, "says the doctor. "Show me what you mean."

The woman touches her elbow and screams in agony. She then touches her knee and screams, and then pushes on her ankle and screams.

"Just as I thought," says the doctor. "You have a broken finger."

Q: Why did the blonde plant Cheerios in her garden?

A: She thought they were donut seeds.

Two men are fishing on a riverbank when they see a funeral

procession passing by. One of the men stands up, takes off his hat, and bows.

"That was a very nice thing to do," says the second man.

"Well," says the first, "we were married for 25 years."

"I've been told we only use 10% of our brains, imagine if we could learn to use the other 60%."

A redhead, a brunette, and a blonde are in a bar when the bartender tells them about a magic mirror in the ladies' room. Apparently, he says, the mirror gives rewards if you stare into it and say something true. But if you lie, you're sucked into the mirror and never heard from again.

So the redhead heads to the bathroom, looks into the mirror, and says, "I think I'm the most beautiful woman in this bar." A million dollars suddenly appears before her.

Then the brunette heads into the bathroom, looks into the mirror, and says, "I think I'm the smartest woman in this bar." The key to a new Ferrari materializes in her fingers.

Then the blonde goes in, looks into the mirror, and begins, "I think..." And she's sucked in and never heard from again.

A guy hears a knock at his door. When he answers it, there's nobody there, but there's a snail on the welcome mat. Frustrated, the guy picks up the snail and hurls it into the street.

Five years go by, and there's another knock at the door. The man answers it, and again there's no one standing there. But there's a snail on the welcome mat. The snail looks up and says, "What was that all about?"

Alcohol and calculus don't mix. Never drink and derive.

Two guys decide to go bungee jumping in Mexico. Having never seen bungee jumping before, a crowd of locals gathers to watch. The first guy jumps and when he bounces back up, he's got cuts and bruises all over his face. The second guy helps him back onto the bridge. "What happened," he says. "Was the cord too long?"

"The cord was fine," he gasps, "It was the crowd. What's a piñata?"

My Grandmother once reflected that she wishes she could go back in time when...

-Decisions were made by going "eeny-meeny-miney-mo."

-Mistakes were corrected by simply exclaiming, "do over!"

-"Race issue" meant arguing about who ran the fastest.

- Money issues were handled by whoever was the banker in "Monopoly."

-Catching the fireflies could happily occupy an entire evening.

-It wasn't odd to have two or three "best friends."

-Being old referred to anyone over 20.

-The net on a tennis court was the perfect height to play volleyball and rules didn't matter.

- It was magic when dad would "remove" his thumb.

- It was unbelievable that dodge ball wasn't an Olympic event.

- Having a weapon in school meant being caught with a slingshot.

- Scrapes and bruises were kissed and made better.

- It was a big deal to finally be tall enough to ride the "big people" rides at the amusement park.

- Getting a foot of snow was a dream come true.

- Abilities were discovered because of a "double-dog-dare."

- Saturday morning cartoons weren't 30-minute ads for action figures.

- "Oly-oly-oxen-free" made perfect sense.

-Spinning around, getting dizzy and falling down was cause for giggles.

-The worst embarrassment was being picked last for a team.

-War was a card game.

-Water balloons were the ultimate weapon.

-Baseball cards in the spokes transformed any bike into a motorcycle.

-Taking drugs meant orange-flavored chewable aspirin.

A wife sees a daytime talk show where they're discussing remarriage after a spouse passes away. After chatting with her mother and friends about it at length, she asks her husband later that night in bed, "Honey, if I were to die, would you remarry?"

He replies, "Well, after a considerable period of grieving and maybe even therapy...we all need companionship. So, I guess I would."

Spurred on by her husband's response, she then asks, "If I died and you remarried, would you let the woman live in this house?"

He replies, "We've spent a lot of money getting this house just the way we want it. It seems like a waste to give it all up...so, yes, I guess I would."

Looking flustered, the wife finally asks, "Would you let her use my golf clubs?"

"Oh no...she's left handed."

It's October, and an Indian chief thinks it's going to be a cold winter. So he instructs his tribe to collect wood.

To double-check his prediction, the chief calls the National Weather Service and asks a meteorologist if the winter is going to be a cold one.

The man responds, "According to our indicators, we think it might."

So the chief tells his people to find extra wood, just in case. A week later he calls the National Weather Service again, and they confirm that a harsh winter is headed their way.

The chief orders all his people to scavenge every scrap of wood they can. Two weeks later he calls the National Weather Service again and asks, "Are you absolutely sure this winter is going to be very cold?"

"Absolutely," the man replies. "The Indians are collecting wood like crazy."

"He who laughs last thinks slowest."

This guy runs home and bursts in yelling, "Pack your bags, honey. I just won the lottery!"

She says, "Oh, wonderful! Should I pack for the beach or the mountains?"

He replies, "I don't care...just get out!"

"I can't stand it when people start something and don't fi

A ventriloquist is touring clubs in Florida. With his dummy on his knee, he's going through his usual dumb blonde jokes when a blonde woman in the audience stands on her chair and shouts, "I've heard enough of your stupid blonde jokes. What does the color of a person's hair have to do with her worth as a human being? It's guys like you who keep women like me from being respected at work, and from reaching our full potential!"

The embarrassed ventriloquist starts to apologize, when the blonde yells, "You stay out of this, mister! I'm talking to that little guy sittin' on your knee!"

Be nice to your kids. They'll choose your nursing home.

A brother and sister are talking to each other when the little boy gets up and walks over to his grandfather. "Make a frog noise, Grandpa," he says.

"Why?" asks the grandfather.

"Please, please make a frog noise," pleads the boy.

"Not unless you tell me why."

"Because Mommy said when you croak we can all go to Disneyworld."

Always remember you're unique, just like everyone else.

Brian gets a parrot for his birthday. It has a bad attitude and a worse vocabulary. Every other word is offensive. Brian tries to change the bird's behavior with polite words, soft music...but nothing works. Out of desperation, he throws the bird in the freezer. It squawks, kicks, screams, and then falls silent. Brian, worried, swings the freezer door open. The parrot calmly steps out. "I believe I may have offended you with my rude language and actions. I will endeavor at once to correct my behavior."

Brian is amazed at the change in the bird's attitude and is about to ask what caused it when the parrot continues, "May I ask what the chicken did?"

A woman goes into a funeral home to make arrangements for her husband. She tells the director she'd like him to be buried in a dark blue suit.

"Wouldn't it be easier to bury him in the black suit he is wearing?" he asks. But she insists on dark blue and gives him a blank check to buy one with.

The woman returns for the wake later that day and sees her husband in the coffin wearing a dark blue suit.

"It's beautiful, " she says. "How much did it cost?"

"Nothing," says the director. "After you left, a corpse with a blue suit was brought in. They were about the same size so I asked his widow if she would mind if her husband was buried in a black suit. She said fine, so...I switched the heads."

A genii offers to grant a man one wish.

"Build me a bridge to Hawaii, " says the man, "so I can drive over anytime."

The genii says, "Think of the logistics of that kind of undertaking. The supports to reach to the bottom of the Pacific. The concrete and steel it would take. I can do this, of course, but it's hard for me to justify your desire for worldly things. Take a little time and think of another wish."

The man thinks for a while and says, "I wish I could understand women."

After a moment, the genii says, "You want two lanes or four?"

A little man walks into a biker bar and clears his throat. "Um, which of you gentlemen owns the Doberman tied to the parking meter?"

A big biker turns slowly on his stool, "It's mine. Why?"

"Well," squeaks the little man, "I believe my dog just killed it."

"What?" bellows the biker in disbelief. "What kind of dog you got than can take down my Doberman?"

"Sir," answers the little man meekly, "it's a Chihuahua."

"A Chihuahua! A Chihuahua?" shouts the biker. "How could a little Chihuahua kill a Doberman?"

"Well, it appears that he choked on it, sir."

Three guys die in a car crash and meet St. Peter.

"When you're in your casket and your friends and family are gathered around, what would you like to hear them say?" St. Peter asks.

"I'd like to hear someone say I made a difference," answers the first guy.

"I'd like to hear someone say I was a good family man, " answers the second guy.

"And you?" St. Peter asks the third guy.

"I guess I'd like to hear someone say, 'Look! He's moving!'"

Radio conversation released by the chief of naval operations 10.10.95...

Americans: Please divert your course 15 degrees to the north to avoid a collision.

Canadians: Recommend you divert YOUR course 15 degrees to the south to avoid a collision.

Americans: This is the captain of a US Navy ship. I say again, divert YOUR course.

Canadians: No, I say again divert YOUR course.

Americans: THIS IS THE AIRCRAFT CARRIER USS ENTERPRISE; WE ARE A LARGE WARSHIP OF THE US NAVY. DIVERT YOUR COURSE NOW.

Canadians: This is Rocky Point Lighthouse. Your call.

Farmer Joe is suing a trucking company over injuries he suffered in an auto accident. The company's layer begins to cross-examine the plaintiff.

"Isn't it true you said, 'I'm fine,' at the scene of the accident?" asks the lawyer.

"Well, I'll tell you what happened," farmer Joes starts.

"Did you or did you not say, 'I'm fine!'" thunders the lawyer.

"Let me explain," pleads the farmer. "I had just loaded my mule Daisy into the trailer and was driving down the highway when this semi-truck crashed into us. I was hurt real bad. When the highway patrolman came on the scene, he heard Daisy moaning and groaning. He took one look at her, pulled out his gun, and shot her between the eyes.

Then he came across the road with his gun in hand, looked at me, and said, "Your mule was in such bad shape I had to shoot her. How are you?"

"I've been thinking about this a lot lately, and I'm pretty sure my favorite Wookie is Chewbacca."

An elderly man in Miami calls his son, Dave, in New York and says, "I hate to ruin your day, but your mother and I are divorcing. Forty years of misery is enough! I'm sick of her, and I'm sick of talking about this so call your sister in

Chicago and tell her," and then hangs up.

The son frantically calls his sister, who goes nuts upon hearing the news.

She calls her father and yells, "You are NOT getting a divorce! Dave and I will be there tomorrow. Until then, don't do a single thing, do you hear me?"

The father hangs up the phone, turns to his wife, and says, "It worked! The kids are coming for a visit, and they are paying their own way!"

A man walks into a bar, sits down and orders a drink. He says "Give me a drink before problems start!" The bartender doesn't understand but gives the man a drink.

After 15 minutes the man orders a drink again saying "Give me a drink before problems start!" The bartender looks a little bit confused but pours the man a drink.

This goes on the whole night and after the 15th drink the bartender is totally confused and asks the man "What do you mean with before problems start? And when are you going to pay for all the drinks you drunk."

The man answers "You see, now the problems start!"

Two friends get lost during a hiking trip through the desert. Several days later, they are dehydrated and near death.

Out of nowhere, they see a tree in the distance that appears to be covered with bacon. One guy sprints ahead, only to be gunned down in a hail of gunfire.

"Run!" the dying man yells out. "It's not a bacon tree. It's a ham bush!"

Q: How many psychiatrists does it take to change a light bulb?

A: One, but the bulb has got to want to change itself.

A guy walks into the doctor's office with a banana stuck in one ear, a cucumber in the other and a strawberry wedged in his nostrils.

"Doc, I need help," says the guy. "Something's wrong with me."

"Well," says the doctor, "I can see you're not eating right."

"I hate it when I accidentally use the same word too many times in a sentence accidentally."

A man takes his Rottweiler to the veterinarian and says, "My dog is going cross-eyed. Is there anything you can do to help him?"

"Well," replies the vet, "let's have a look at him." So he picks up the dog and checks its eyes.

After a quick exam, the vet turns to the owner and says, "I'm afraid I'm going to have to put him down."

"Why? Just because he's cross-eyed?"

"No," says the vet, "It's just that he's really heavy!"

Actual Call Center Calls

Customer: "I've been calling 700-1000 for two days and can't get through; can you help?"
Operator: "Where did you get that number, sir?"
Customer: "It's on the door of your business."
Operator: "Sir, those are the hours that we're open."

Caller: "Can you give me the telephone number for Jack?"
Operator: "I'm sorry, sir, I don't understand who you are talking about."
Caller: "On page 1, section 5, of the user guide it clearly states that I need to unplug the fax machine from the AC wall socket and telephone Jack before cleaning.

Now, can you give me the number for Jack?"
Operator: "I think it means the telephone plug on the wall."

Directory Enquiries
Caller: "I'd like the number of the Argo Fish Bar, please."
Operator: "I'm sorry, there's no listing. Are you sure that the spelling is correct?"
Caller: "Well, it used to be called the Bargo Fish Bar but the 'B' fell off."

Then there was the caller who asked for a knitwear company in Woven.
Operator: "Woven? Are you sure?"
Caller: "Yes. That's what it says on the label -- Woven in Scotland."

On another occasion, a man making heavy breathing sounds from a phone box told a worried operator: "I haven't got a pen, so I'm steaming up the window to write the number on."

Tech Support: "I need you to right-click on the Open Desktop."
Customer: "OK."
Tech Support: "Did you get a pop-up menu?"
Customer: "No."
Tech Support: "OK. Right-Click again. Do you see a pop-up menu?"
Customer: "No."
Tech Support: "OK, sir. Can you tell me what you have done up until this point?"
Customer: "Sure. You told me to write 'click' and I wrote 'click'."
Tech Support: "OK. At the bottom

left hand side of your screen, can you see the 'OK' button displayed?"

Customer: "Wow! How can you see my screen from there?"

Tech Support: "OK, the computer should be telling you to press any key."

Customer: ....

Tech Support: "Let me know when you are ready to move on."

Customer: "I keep looking and looking and I can't find the "any key"."

Tech Support: "Now, to install the program, we need to insert the CD."

Customer: "And where do I do that?"

Tech Support: "The CD drive in the front of your computer, push the eject button and the tray should open."

Customer: "CD player? I've been using that as a cup holder!"

Tech Support: "Press the left button on your computer mouse to continue."

Customer: "I'm trying but my toe won't reach."

Tech Support: "Your toe?"

Customer; "Yes, I thought you used the mouse like my sewing machine peddle, am I doing it wrong?"

A blonde walks into a library, goes up to the front desk, and says, "I'm here to see the doctor."

"This is a library, dearie," says the librarian.

"Oh, I'm sorry," whispers the blonde. "I'm here to see the doctor."

A married couple is walking past their neighbors' house. "Dave and Linda are so loving toward each other," says the wife. "Every time he sees her, he gives her a big kiss...unlike someone I know."

"Hey, I'd love to," says the husband. "But I don't know her that well."

Did you hear about the dyslexic agnostic insomniac?

He stayed awake all night wondering if there really was a dog.

    A man and a woman were having dinner in a fine restaurant. Their waitress, taking another order at a table a few paces away, noticed that the man was slowly sliding down his chair and under the table, with the woman acting unconcerned.

    The waitress watched as the man slid all the way down his chair and out of sight under the table. Still, the woman dining across from him appeared calm and unruffled, apparently unaware that her dining companion had disappeared.

    After the waitress finished taking the order, she came over to the table and said to the woman, "Pardon me, ma'am, but I think your husband just slid under the table."

The woman calmly looked up at her and replied firmly, "No he didn't. He just walked in the door."

ATTORNEY: She had three children, right?
WITNESS: Yes.
ATTORNEY: How many were boys?
WITNESS: None.
ATTORNEY: Were there any girls?

ATTORNEY: How was your first marriage terminated?
WITNESS: By death.
ATTORNEY: And by whose death was it terminated?

ATTORNEY: Can you describe the individual?
WITNESS: He was about medium height and had a beard.
ATTORNEY: Was this a male or a female?

ATTORNEY: Is your appearance here this morning pursuant to a deposition notice which I sent to your attorney?
WITNESS: No, this is how I dress when I go to work.

ATTORNEY: ALL your responses MUST be oral, OK? What school did you go to?
WITNESS: Oral.

A blonde is on a date with a geography teacher. "Believe it or not, I know all the state capitals," she says proudly.

"Oh, yeah?" says the guy. "What's the capital of Wisconsin?"

"That's easy," she replies. "It's a W."

A general is giving the president his daily briefing. He concludes by saying: "Yesterday, 3 Brazilian soldiers were killed in an accident"

"OH NO!" the President exclaims. "That's terrible!"

His staff sits stunned at this display of emotion, nervously watching as the President sits, head in hands. Finally he looks up and asks.......... "How many is a Brazillion??!'

"I hate it when people misspell obviuos words."

Sherlock Holmes and Dr. Watson go on a camping trip, set up their tent, and fall asleep. Some hours later, Holmes wakes his faithful friend.

"Watson, look up at the sky and tell me what you see."

Watson replies, "I see millions of stars."

"What does that tell you?"

Watson ponders for a minute. "Astronomically speaking, it tells me that there are millions of galaxies and potentially billions of planets. Astrologically, it tells me that Saturn is in Leo. Time wise, it appears to be approximately a quarter past three. Theologically, it's evident the Lord is all-powerful and we are small and insignificant. Meteorologically, it seems we will have a beautiful day tomorrow. What does it tell you?"

Holmes is silent for a moment, and then speaks. "Watson, you idiot, someone has stolen our tent."

Q: What do you call a musician without a girlfriend?

A: Homeless.

Q: Where's the English Channel?

A: I don't know - our television doesn't pick it up.

Life lessons from my Grandfather

1. Trouble in marriage often starts when a man gets so busy earnin' his salt that he forgets his sugar.

2. Too many couples marry for better, or for worse, but not for good.

3. When a man marries a woman, they become one; but the trouble starts when they try to decide which one.

4. If a man has enough horse sense to treat his wife like a thoroughbred, she will never turn into a nag.

5. On anniversaries, the wise husband always forgets the past - but never the present.

6. The bonds of matrimony are a good investment only when the interest is kept up.

7. Many girls like to marry a military man - he can cook, sew, and make beds and is in good health, and he's already used to taking orders.

8. Eventually you will reach a point when you stop lying about your age and start bragging about it.

9. The older we get, the fewer things seem worth waiting in line for.

10. Some people try to turn back their odometers. Not me, I want people to know "why" I look this way. I've traveled a long way and some of the roads weren't paved.

11. How old would you be if you didn't know how old you are?

12. I don't know how I got over the hill without getting to the top.

13. One things no one tells you about aging is that it is such a nice change from being young.

14. Ah, being young is beautiful, but being old is comfortable.

15. Old age is when former classmates are so gray and wrinkled and bald, they don't recognize you.

16. If you don't learn to laugh at trouble, you won't have anything to laugh at when you are old.

Two guys are in a bar.

First one: "My wife is an angel."

Second one: "You're lucky! Mine is still alive."

An English teacher wrote the words, "Woman without her man is nothing" on the blackboard and asked the students to punctuate it so that it made sense.

The boys wrote: "Woman, without her man, is nothing."

The girls wrote: "Woman! Without her, man is nothing."

Just before Thanksgiving Jim and Eddie are out hunting for turkeys when Jim keels over and collapses. He doesn't seem to be breathing and his eyes are glazed. Eddie gets out his cell phone and calls the emergency services.

He gasps, "My friend Jim is dead! What can I do?"

The operator says, "Calm down, I can help. First, let's make sure he's dead."

There's a silence, then a shot is heard.

Back on the phone, Eddie says, "OK, now what?"

A man follows a woman with a parrot out of a movie theater. He stops her and says, "I'm sorry to bother you, but I couldn't help but notice that your bird seemed to understand the movie. He cried at the right spots, he was fidgeting in his seat during the boring parts, and he laughed at the jokes. Don't you find that unusual?"

"I do indeed," she replies. "He hated the book."

One day a teacher was giving a lecture on philosophy, and had the class enthralled. It was a brilliant lecture.

Suddenly, over his head a bright light flashed and a genii appeared and approached the teacher.

She said, "You are doing such a good job teaching this class, I have decided to give you one wish. You can have infinite money, infinite wisdom, or infinite knowledge."

Thinking for a minute, he humbly asked for infinite wisdom. She tapped him with a magic wand and disappeared in a flash. The class came forward to hear the first words from a man with infinite wisdom.

He said, "It would have been wiser to take the money..."

A man tells his doctor he's unable to do all the things around the house that he used to do. After the exam, he says, "Now, doc, I can take it. Tell me in plain English what is wrong with me."

"In layman's terms, you're lazy," says the doctor.

"Ok, now give me a medical term, so I can tell my wife."

Charles Dickens walks into a bar and orders a Martini.

The bartender says "Olive or Twist?"

A foolproof method for sculpting an elephant: get a huge block of marble, and then chip away everything that doesn't look like an elephant.

Grandma reflects on living in the 60s VS. being over 60

Then: Long hair.
Now: Longing for hair.

Then: Moving to California because it's cool.
Now: Moving to California because it's warm.

Then: Trying to look like Marlon Brando or Elizabeth Taylor.

Now: Trying not to look like Marlon Brando or Elizabeth Taylor.

Then: Getting out to a new, hip joint.
Now: Getting a new hip joint.

Then: Rolling Stones.
Now: Kidney stones.

Then: Peace sign.
Now: Mercedes logo.

Then: Passing the driver's test.
Now: Passing the vision test.

Then: "Whatever"
Now: "Depends"

A man returns from Africa feeling very ill. He visits his doctor, who immediately rushes the guy to the Mayo Clinic.

The man wakes up to the ringing of a telephone in a stark room at the hospital and answers it. "We've received the results from your tests," says the doctor on the other end of the line. "Bad news, you have Ebola."

"Oh, my," cries the man. "Doc! What am I going to do?""

"Don't' worry. First, we're going to put you on a diet of pizza, pancakes, and pita bread." Says the doctor.

"Will that cure me?"

"No, but it's the only food we'll be able to get under the door."

Bacon and Eggs walk into a bar...

The bartender says "Sorry, we don't serve breakfast."

A frog telephones the Psychic Hotline and is told, "You're going to meet a beautiful young girl who will want to know everything about you."

The frog says, "This is great! Will I meet her at a party or what?"

"No," says the psychic, "next term in her biology lesson."

A passenger train is creeping along, slowly. Finally it creaks to a halt. A passenger sees a conductor walking by outside. "What's going on?" she yells out the window. "Cow on the track!" replies the conductor.

Ten minutes later the train resumes its slow pace. Within five minutes, however, it stops again. The woman sees the same conductor walk again.

She leans out the window and yells, "What happened? Did we catch up with the cow again?"

An artist asked the gallery owner if there had been any interest in his paintings on display at that time.

"I have good news and bad news," the owner replied, "the good news is that a gentleman enquired about your work and wondered if it would appreciate in value after your death.

When I told him it would, he bought all 15 of your paintings."

"That's wonderful," the artist exclaimed, "what's the bad news?"

"The guy was your doctor..."

A businessman enters a tavern, sits down at the bar, and orders a double martini on the rocks.

After he finishes the drink, he peeks inside his shirt pocket, and orders another double martini. After he finishes that one, he peeks inside his shirt pocket again and orders yet another double martini.

The bartender says, "Look, buddy, I'll bring ya' martinis all night long - but you gotta tell me why you look inside your shirt pocket before you order a refill."

The customer replies, "I'm peeking at a photo of my wife. When she starts to look good, I know it's time to go home."

Two guys are talking while sitting on a bench in the park. "All of my ancestors followed the medical profession." said the first.

"Doctors?" queried the second.

"Nope. Undertakers and lawyers."

The new employee stood before the paper shredder looking confused.

"Need some help?" a secretary, walking by, asked.

"Yes," he replied, "how does this thing work?"

"Simple," she said, taking the fat report from his hand and feeding it into the shredder.

"Thanks, but where do the copies come out?"

Q: What is the difference between a Southern zoo and a Northern Zoo?

A: At Southern Zoos the animal descriptions include cooking times.

Humor in Church

Q. What kind of man was Boaz before he married Ruth?

A. Ruthless.

Q. What do they call pastors in Germany?

A. German Shepherds.

Q. Who was the greatest financier in the Bible?

A. Noah. He was floating his stock while everyone else was in liquidation.

Q. Who was the greatest female financier in the Bible?

A. Pharaoh's daughter. She went down to the bank of the Nile and drew out a little prophet.

Q. What kind of motor vehicles are

in the Bible?

A. Jehovah drove Adam and Eve out of the Garden in a Fury. David's Triumph was heard throughout the land. Also, probably a Honda, because the apostles were all in one Accord.

Q. Who was the greatest comedian in the Bible?

A. Samson. He brought the house down.

Q. What excuse did Adam give to his children as to why he no longer lived in Eden ?

A. Your mother ate us out of house and home.

Q. Which servant of God was the most flagrant law breaker in the Bible?

A. Moses. He broke all 10

commandments at once.

Q. Which area of Palestine was especially wealthy?

A. The area around Jordan. The banks were always overflowing.

Q. Who is the greatest babysitter mentioned in the Bible?

A. David. He rocked Goliath to a very deep sleep.

Q. Which Bible character had no parents?

A. Joshua, son of Nun.

Q. Why didn't they play cards on the Ark?

A. Because Noah was standing on the deck.

Did you know it's a sin for a woman to make coffee? Yup, it's in the Bible. It says. . 'He-brews'

There were two men in a building site. One of them said, "Can you help me find my ear?"

The other one, holding up an ear, asked, "Is this it?"

"No" replied the first one, "mine has a pencil behind it."

Q: How many visitors to an art gallery does it take to change a light bulb?

A: Two. One to do it, and one to say "Huh! My four-year old could've done that!"

"If there are any idiots in the room, will they please stand up," said the sarcastic teacher. After a long silence, one freshman rose to his feet.

"Now then, mister, why do you consider yourself an idiot?" enquired the teacher with a sneer.

"Well, actually I don't," said the student, "but I hate to see you standing up there all by yourself."

Christopher Columbus was the best deal-maker in history. He left not knowing where he was going, and upon arriving, not knowing where he was. He returned not knowing where he had been, and did it all on borrowed money.

A worker was called to the office by his supervisor for talking back to his foreman.

Supervisor: "Is it true that you called him a liar?"

Worker: "Yes, I did."

Supervisor: "Did you call him stupid?"

Worker: "Yes."

Supervisor: "And did you call him an opinionated, bullheaded egomaniac?"

Worker: "No, but would you write that down so I can remember it?"

A bald man took a seat in a beauty shop. "How can I help you?" asked the stylist.

"I went for a hair transplant," the guy explained, "but I couldn't stand the pain. If you can make my hair look like yours without causing me any discomfort, I'll pay you $5000."

"No problem," said the stylist and she quickly shaved her head.

A man walks into a bar, sits down and says to the girl next to him, "Hey, you want to hear a great blonde joke?"

"Listen, buddy," the girl replies. "You can surely tell that I AM blonde. My two friends here are both world ranked judo masters and they're blonde too. Now, do you still want to tell that joke?"

"Nah," the man replies, "I don't feel like explaining it three times."

Two cannibals are eating a clown. One says to the other, "Hey, does this taste funny to you?"

A cop pulls over a couple for speeding. He walks up to the driver and says, "I clocked you doing 80 mph, sir."

"Gee, officer," says the driver, "I had it on cruise control at 60."

"Don't be silly, dear," the wife chimes in. "This car doesn't have cruise control."

As the cop begins to write the ticket, the husband growls to his wife, "Can't you just keep your mouth shut?"

The wife smiles and says, "You should be happy the radar detector went off when it did."

"A radar detector, eh?" says the officer. "Those are illegal in this state." He starts to write up a second ticket.

"Will you please keep your mouth shut!" screams the husband to the wife.

The officer bends down, looks at the woman and asks, "Does he always talk to you like that?"

"Oh, heavens no," she replies, "Only when he's been drinking."

Two elderly couples are playing bridge, and at one point the wives go into the kitchen. One of the gentlemen says, "Last night we went to a really fantastic restaurant. I highly recommend it."

"What is the name of it?" the other man asks.

The first man thinks for a while and finally says, "Hey, what's the name of that flower? You know, it's red and has thorns on its stem."

"You mean a rose?"

"Yeah, that's it." He turns toward the kitchen and yells, "Rose, what's the name of that restaurant we went to last night?"

A man joins a Tibetan temple. He takes a vow of silence but is allowed to say two words every year.

After a long 12 months of eating rice, sleeping on a wooden bed with an old blanket, and working 14 hours a day in the fields, the man goes to the head monk and says, "More blankets."

Another year passes, and he visits the head monk and says, "More food."

The man goes through one more year eating good meals and sleeping well, but he's drained by the long workdays. He calls on the head monk uses his two words to say, "I'm leaving."

"Good," the head monk replies. "You've done nothing but complain since you got here."

Late one night a guy is showing some friends around his brand new apartment.

The last stop is the bedroom, where a big brass gong sits next to the bed.

"What's that gong for?" the friend asks him.

"It's not a gong," the man replies, "It's a talking clock."

"How does it work?"

The guy picks up a hammer, gives the gong an ear shattering whack and steps back.

Suddenly, someone on the other side of the wall in the next apartment screams, "For goodness sake, you jerk...it's 3:30 in the morning!"

"What time does the library open?" the man on the phone asked.

"Nine A.M." came the reply. "And what's the idea of calling me at home in the middle of the night to ask a question like that?"

"Not until nine A.M.?" the man asked in a disappointed voice.

"No, not till nine A.M.!" the librarian said. "Why do you want to get in before nine A.M.?"

"Who said I wanted to get in?" the man sighed sadly. "I want to get out."

A man walks into a bar, and orders a drink. As he sits there, the jar of nuts on the bar tells him what a nice shirt he is wearing. Disturbed by this, he reaches for the pay phone. As he approaches the phone, it starts screaming and shouting at him.

He runs to the bar and explains this to the barman. The barman apologizes and says, "The peanuts are complimentary, but the pay phone is out of order!"

Signs that you have grown up

1. Dinner and a movie is the whole date instead of the beginning of one.

2. You actually eat breakfast food at breakfast time.

3. Eating a basket of chicken wings at 3 AM now severely upsets, rather than settles, your stomach.

4. 6:00 AM is when you get up, not when you go to bed.

5. You hear your favorite song on an elevator.

6. You watch the Weather Channel.

7. Your friends marry and divorce instead of date and break up.

8. You go from 130 days of vacation time to 14.

9. Jeans and a sweater no longer qualify as "dressed up".

10. You're the one calling the police because those kids next door won't turn down the stereo.

11. Your car insurance goes down and car payments go up.

12. You feed your dog Science Diet instead of McDonald's leftovers.

13. Sleeping on the couch makes your back hurt.

14. You no longer take naps from noon to 6 PM!

A lady inserted an 'ad' in the classifieds: "Husband wanted".

Next day she received a hundred letters. They all said the same thing: "You can have mine."

The village blacksmith finally found an apprentice willing to work hard at low pay for long hours. The blacksmith immediately began his instructions to the lad: "When I take the shoe out of the fire, I'll lay it on the anvil; and when I nod my head, you hit it with this hammer."

The apprentice did just as he was told. Now *he's* the village blacksmith.

Q: How many artists does it take to change a light bulb?

A: Ten. One to change it, and nine to reassure him about how good it looks.

A man speaks frantically into the phone, "My wife is pregnant, and her contractions are only two minutes apart!"

"Is this her first child?" the doctor queries.

"No, you idiot!" the man shouts. "This is her husband!"

A housewife, an accountant and a lawyer were asked, "How much is 2+2?"

The housewife replies: "Four!"

The accountant says: "I think it's either 3 or 4. Let me run those figures through my spreadsheet one more time."

The lawyer pulls the drapes, dims the lights and asks in a hushed voice, "How much do you want it to be?"

A woman and her little girl were visiting the grave of the little girl's grandmother. On their way through the cemetery back to the car, the little girl asked, "Mommy, do they ever bury two people in the same grave?"

"Of course not, dear." replied the mother, "Why would you think that?"

"The tombstone back there said 'Here lies a lawyer and an honest man.'"

"Doctor, Doctor, You've got to help me - I just can't stop my hands shaking!"

"Do you drink a lot?"

"Not really - I spill most of it!"

An applicant was asked if he was familiar with any machines. He said "Four."

"That's great. What are the four machines?"

He said, "Coke, coffee, candy, and cigarette."

After surgery, the surgeon told his patient: "I'm afraid we're going to have to open you back up. Because, you see, I forgot my rubber gloves inside you."

Patient: "Well, if that's all, I'd rather pay for them if you just leave me alone."

Doctor: "I have some bad news and some very bad news."

Patient: "Well, you might as well give me the bad news first."

Doctor: "The lab called with your test results. They said you have 24 hours to live."

Patient: "24 hours! That's terrible!! What could be worse?! What's the very bad news?"

Doctor: "I've been trying to reach you since yesterday."

Ladies, when a woman steals your spouse, there is no better revenge than to let her keep them.

"Doctor" said the patient, "are you sure I'm suffering from pneumonia? I once heard of a doctor treating someone with pneumonia -- and finally he died of typhus."

"Don't worry, that won't happen to me", the doctor replied. "If I treat someone with pneumonia he'll die of pneumonia."

A guy walks into work, and both of his ears are all bandaged up. The boss says, "What happened to your ears?"

He says, "Yesterday I was ironing a shirt when the phone rang and pshhhhh! I accidentally answered the iron."

The boss says, "Well, that explains one ear, but what happened to your other ear?"

He says, "Well, jeez, then I had to call the doctor!"

The woman applying for work in a Florida lemon grove seemed way too qualified for the job.

Foreman: "Look Miss, have you any actual experience in picking lemons?"

Woman: "Well, as a matter of fact, yes! I've been divorced three times."

Dear Christopher,

I know you joke about having A.D.D. so I thought I would email you about a condition I call A. A. A. D. D. - Age Activated Attention Deficit Disorder

This is how it manifests:

I decide to water my garden. As I turn on the hose in the driveway, I look over at my dirty ol' Pontiac and decide it needs washing. As I start toward the garage, I notice that there is mail on the porch table that I brought up from the mailbox earlier. I decide to go through the mail before I wash the car. I lay the car keys down on the table, put the junk mail in the garbage can under the table, and notice that the can is full. So, I decide to put the bills back on the table and take out the garbage first. But then I think, since I'm going to be near the mailbox when I take out the garbage anyway, I may as well pay the bills first. I take my checkbook off the table, and see that there is only one check left. My extra checks are in my desk in the study, so I go inside the house to my desk where I find the can of Diet Coke that I had been drinking. I'm going to look for my checks, but first I need to push the Diet Coke aside so that I don't accidentally knock it over. I see that the pop is getting warm, and I decide I should put it in the refrigerator to keep it cold. As I head toward the kitchen with the Diet Coke, a vase of flowers on the counter catches my eye--they need to be watered. I set the Diet Coke down on the counter, and I discover my reading glasses that I've been searching for all morning. I decide I better put them back on my desk, but first I'm going to water the flowers. I set the glasses back down on the counter, fill a container with water and suddenly I spot the TV remote. Someone left it on the kitchen table. I realize that tonight when we go to watch TV, I will be looking for the remote, but I won't remember that it's on the kitchen table, so I decide to put it back in the den where it belongs, but first I'll water the flowers. I pour some water in the flowers, but quite a bit of it spills on the floor. So, I set the remote back down on the table, get some towels and wipe up the spill. Then I head down the hall trying to remember what I was planning to do.

At the end of the day:

* the car isn't washed

* the bills aren't paid

* there is a warm can of Diet Coke sitting on the counter

* the flowers don't have enough water

* there is still only one check in my check book

* I can't find the remote

* I can't find my glasses

* I don't remember what I did with the car keys.

Then when I try to figure out why nothing got done today, I'm really baffled because I know I was busy all day long, and I'm really tired. I realize this is a serious problem, and I'll try to get some help for it, but first I'll send Christopher an e-mail.

After a quarrel, a husband said to his wife, "You know, I was a fool when I married you."

She replied, "Yes, dear, but I was in love and didn't notice."

Man is incomplete until he is married. Then he is finished.

A woman was telling her friend, "It is I who made my husband a millionaire."

"And what was he before you married him?" her friend asked.

"A billionaire" she replied.

The young lady, upon her engagement, went to her mother and said, "I've found a man just like father!"

Her mother replied, "So what do you want from me, sympathy?"

A little boy asked his father "Daddy, how much does it cost to get married?"

And the father replied, "I don't know son, I'm still paying."

I want to die in my sleep like my grandfather...not screaming and yelling like the passengers in his car...

Young Son: "Is it true, Dad, I heard that in some parts of Africa a man doesn't know his wife until he marries her?"

Father: "That happens in every country, son."

"I never knew what real happiness was until I got married; and then it was too late."

Q. What's the difference between a run over dog and a run over lawyer?

A. The dog has skid marks before it.

A tourist asks a man in uniform, "Are you a policeman?"

"No, I am an undercover detective."

"So why are you in uniform?"

"Today is my day off."

The most effective way to remember your wife's birthday is to forget it once.

Teacher: "If you reached in your right pocket and found a nickel, and you reached in your left pocket and found another one, what would you have?"

Boy: "Somebody else's pants."

A policeman pulls a man over for speeding and asks him to get out of the car. After looking the man over he says "Sir, I couldn't help but notice your eyes are bloodshot. Have you been drinking?"

The man gets really indignant and says, "Officer, I couldn't help but notice your eyes are glazed. Have you been eating doughnuts?"

A policeman stops a lady and asks for her license.

Policeman: "Lady, it says here that you should be wearing glasses."

Woman: "Well, I have contacts."

Policeman: "I don't care who you know! You're still getting a ticket!"

One evening a man arrived home from work and found his wife waiting for him at the front door.

"I want you to take me somewhere expensive tonight," she said.

"No problem, honey," the man replied. " I know just the place."

"So," his wife asked as they were pulling out of their driveway, "where are we going?"

"The gas station," he replied.

A woman's husband had been slipping in and out of a coma for several months, but she dutifully stayed by his bedside every single day. One afternoon, he finally opened his eyes. When he did, he looked at his wife and said, "You've always been with me through the bad times. When I got fired, you were there to support me. When my business failed, you were there. When I got hot, you were by my side. When we lost the house, you stayed with me, and when my health started failing, you were still by my side. So you know what?"

"What dear?" his wife asked, smiling bravely.

"I think you're really bad luck," he said.

A husband and wife were dining out together when the wife noticed that her husband kept staring at an attractive woman who was sitting at the bar throwing back drink after drink.

"Do you know that woman?" she asked.

"Yes," her husband replied. "She's an ex-girlfriend. She started drinking after we broke up, and apparently she hasn't been sober since."

"My goodness!" his wife exclaimed. "Who'd have thought a person could celebrate for that long?"

"Dad, can you write in the dark?"

"I think so. What is it you want me to write?"

"Your name on this report card."

Wisdom From My Grandmother

1. If you're too open minded, your brains will fall out.

2. Age is a very high price to pay for maturity.

3. Going to church doesn't make you a Christian any more than going to a garage makes you a mechanic.

4. Artificial intelligence is no match for natural stupidity.

5. If you must choose between two evils, pick the one you've never tried before.

6. My idea of housework is to sweep the room with a glance.

7. Not one shred of evidence supports the notion that life is serious.

8. It is easier to get forgiveness than permission.

9. For every action, there is an equal and opposite government program.

10. If you look like your passport picture, you probably need the trip.

11. Bills travel through the mail at twice the speed of checks.

12. A conscience is what hurts when all your other parts feel so good.

13. Eat well, stay fit, and die anyway.

14. Men are from earth. Women are from earth. Deal with it.

15. No husband has ever been shot while doing the dishes.

16. A balanced diet is a cookie in each hand.

17. Middle age is when broadness of the mind and narrowness of the waist change places.

18. Opportunities always look bigger going than coming.

19. Junk is something you've kept for years and throw away three weeks before you need it.

20. There is always one more imbecile than you counted on.

21. Experience is a wonderful thing. It enables you to recognize a mistake when you make it again.

22. By the time you can make ends meet, they move the ends.

23. Thou shalt not weigh more than thy refrigerator.

24. Blessed are they who can laugh at themselves for they shall never cease to be amused.

Where in the nursery rhyme does say that Humpty Dumpty is an egg?

Teacher: "Johnny, what is the outside of a tree called?"

Johnny: "I don't know."

Teacher: "Bark, Johnny, bark!"

Johnny: "Woof, woof..!"

So ya know, I've been taking these kung-fu classes lately. I must say they're great. They teach you how to be as powerful as a tiger, as quick as a monkey, and as smart as a dragon. Just the other day, these guys came up to me with a knife and demanded money. So, I turned into a chicken and ran!

A man wrote a letter to a small hotel he planned to visit on his vacation: "I would very much like to bring my dog with me. He is well groomed and very well behaved. Would you be willing to permit me to keep him in my room with me at night?"

An immediate reply came from the hotel owner, who said, "I've been operating this hotel for many years. In all that time, I've never had a dog steal towels, bedclothes, silverware or pictures off the walls. I've never had to evict a dog in the middle of the night for being disorderly. And I've never had a dog run out on a hotel bill. Yes, indeed, your dog is welcome at my hotel. And, if your dog will vouch for you, you're welcome to stay here, too."

A busload of tourists arrives at Runnymede. They gather around the guide who says, "This is the spot where the barons forced King John to sign the Magna Carta."

A fellow at the front of the crowd asks, "When did that happen?"

"1215," answers the guide.

The man looks at his watch and says, "Darn! Just missed it by a half hour!"

Teacher: "You know you can't sleep in my class."

Boy: "I know. But maybe if you were just a little quieter, I could."

A man on his deathbed made one final dying request of his wife.

"Darling, promise me you will marry Andrew after I'm gone," he said.

"Of course, honey, anything you want," his wife replied, "but I thought you hated Andrew."

With his last dying breath her husband said, "I do."

How do you make a blonde laugh on Saturday?

Tell her a joke on Wednesday.

The child comes home from his first day at school.

Mother: "What did you learn today?"

Kid: "Not enough. I have to go back tomorrow."

A guy stood over his tee shot for what seemed an eternity, looking up, looking down, measuring the distance, figuring the wind direction and speed. Driving his partner nuts.

Finally his exasperated partner says, "What is taking so long? Hit the ball!"

The guy answers, "My wife is up there watching me from the clubhouse. I want to make this a perfect shot."

"Well, you don't stand a chance of hitting her from here!"

A brunette is trying to get across a river and suddenly she spots a blonde on the other side.

She yells over to the blonde, "Hey, excuse me! How do I get over to the other side?"

After a quick survey of the river, the blonde calls back, "You ARE on the other side!"

An English professor complained to the pet shop proprietor, "The parrot I purchased uses improper language."

"I'm surprised," said the owner. "I've never taught that bird to swear."

"Oh, it isn't that," explained the professor. "But yesterday I heard him split an infinitive."

Two boll weevils grew up in South Carolina. One went to Hollywood and became a famous actor. The other stayed behind in the cotton fields and never amounted to much.

The second one, naturally, became known as the lesser of the two weevils.

Four People

This is a story about four people, named Everybody, Somebody, Anybody, and Nobody.

There was an important job to be done, and Everybody was sure that Somebody would do it.

Anybody could have done it, but Nobody did. Somebody got angry about this, because it was Everybody's job. Everybody thought Anybody could do it, but Nobody realized that Everybody wouldn't do it. It ended up that Everybody blamed Somebody when Nobody did what Anybody could have done!

Knowing that the minister was very fond of cherry brandy, one of the church elders offered to present him with a bottle on one condition... that the Pastor acknowledges receipt of the gift in the church paper.

"Gladly," replied the good man.

When the church magazine came out a few days later, the elder turned at once to the "appreciation" column. There he read: "The minister extends his thanks to Elder Brown for his gift of fruit and for the spirit in which it was given."

I would give my right arm to be ambidextrous.

Top 45 Oxymorons

45. Act naturally

44. Found missing

43. Resident alien

42. Advanced BASIC

41. Genuine imitation

40. Airline Food

39. Good grief

38. Same difference

37. Almost exactly

36. Government organization

35. Sanitary landfill

34. Alone together

33. Legally drunk

32. Silent scream

31. Living dead

30. Small crowd

29. Business ethics

28. Soft rock

27. Butt Head

26. Military Intelligence

25. Software documentation

24. New classic

23. Sweet sorrow

22. Childproof

21. "Now, then ..."

20. Synthetic natural gas

19. Passive aggression

18. Taped live

17. Clearly misunderstood

16. Peace force

15. Extinct Life

14. Temporary tax increase

13. Computer jock

12. Plastic glasses

11. Terribly pleased

10. Computer security

9. Political science

8. Tight slacks

7. Definite maybe

6. Pretty ugly

5. Twelve-ounce pound cake

4. Diet ice cream

3. Working vacation

2. Exact estimate

1. Microsoft Works

    A funeral service is being held for a woman who has just passed away. As the pallbearers are carrying out the casket, they accidentally bump into a wall. Hearing a faint moan from inside, the woman's husband opens the casket and finds that his wife is actually alive!

She dies again, 10 years later, at which point her husband has to go through another funeral. This time when the pallbearers carry the casket toward the door, the husband yells out, "Watch out for the wall!"

A couple drove several miles down a country road, not saying a word after an earlier discussion had led to an argument, and neither wanted to concede their position.

As they passed a barnyard of mules and pigs, the wife sarcastically asked, "Relatives of yours?"

"Yep," the husband replied, "In-laws."

Two old men in a retirement village were sitting in the reading room and one said to the other, "How do you really feel? I mean, you're 75 years old, how do you honestly feel?"

"Honestly, I feel like a newborn baby. I've got no hair, no teeth, and I just peed myself."

I wonder...

1. Why are there interstate highways in Hawaii?

2. What WAS the best thing before sliced bread?

3. What would chairs look like if our knees bent the other way?

4. If you choke a smurf, what color does it turn?

5. If you cross a four-leaf clover with poison ivy, would you get a rash of good luck?

6. What the world be like without theoretical questions?

7. If a no-armed man has a gun, is he armed?

8. If you got into a taxi and the driver starts driving backwards, does she/he owe you money?

9. If con is the opposite of pro, then is Congress the opposite of progress?

10. If you throw a cat out a car window, does it become kitty litter?

Three retirees, each with a hearing loss, were taking a walk one fine March day.

One remarked to the other, "Windy, ain't it?"

"No," the second man replied, "It's Thursday."

The third man chimed in, "So am I. Let's have a coke."

A man sitting through the first quarter of the Super Bowl can't help but notice the conspicuously vacant seat next to the man to the right of him.

Wanting to make polite conversation he leans over to the man and says "Can you believe someone paid all that money for a seat to the Super Bowl and then doesn't show up?"

The man turns to him and says, "That's my wife's seat she recently passed away." "Oh I am so sorry to hear that." the first man said, "didn't anyone else in your family want the ticket?"

The second man never took his eyes from the football game, "Sure, they did, but they're all at the funeral."

Grandchildren don't make a man feel old ... it's the thought that he's married to a grandmother.

I had trouble with the idea of turning 30 and was oversensitive to any signs of advancing age. When I found a prominent gray hair in my bangs, I pointed to my forehead and asked my husband, "Oh no, have you seen this?"

"What?" he asked. "The wrinkles?"

There's this guy who had been lost and walking in the desert for about 2 weeks. One hot day, he sees the home of a missionary. Tired and weak, he crawls up to the house and collapses on the doorstep. The missionary finds him and nurses him back to health. Feeling better, the man asks the missionary for directions to the nearest town.

On his way out the back door, he sees this horse. He goes back into the house and asks the missionary, "Could I borrow your horse and give it back when I reach the town?" The missionary says, "Sure but there is a special thing about this horse. You have to say 'Thank The Lord' to make it go and 'Amen' to make it stop."

Not paying much attention, the man says, "Sure, OK." So he gets on the horse and says, "Thank The Lord" and the horse starts walking. Then he says, "Thank The Lord, Thank The Lord" and the horse starts trotting. Feeling really brave, the man says, "Thank The Lord, Thank The Lord, Thank The Lord, Thank The Lord, Thank The Lord" and the horse just about takes off.

Pretty soon he sees this cliff coming up and he's doing everything he can to make the horse stop. "Whoa, stop, hold on!!!! "Finally he remembers, "Amen!!" and the horse skids to a stop 4 inches from the edge of the cliff.

The man sinks slowly back into the saddle, sighs deeply, and lets out a heartfelt, " Thank The Lord."

Why didn't the lifeguard rescue the drowning hippie?
She was too far out.

While strolling on the beach, a man finds a golden lamp. Rubbing the lamp, he is suddenly confronted by a genii.

"I shall grant you three wishes, but keep in mind, your ex wife shall receive double your wish."

The man thinks carefully and then proceeds to ask for one billion dollars.

"Your wish is granted, plus, your wife in now the recipient of TWO billion dollars."

"Unhappy about this situation, the man thinks carefully and asks to be granted an extra one hundred years of life."

"It is done, and your wife shall now live an additional TWO hundred years."

Frustrated, the man looks the genii straight in the face, "I want you to scare me half to death."

A retired man who volunteers to entertain patients in nursing homes and hospitals went to one local hospital in Brooklyn and took his portable keyboard along. He told some jokes and sang some funny songs at patients' bedsides.

When he finished he said, in farewell, "I hope you get better."

One elderly gentleman replied, "I hope you get better too."

"I hold an OCD meeting at my house every second Tuesday. I don't have OCD, it's just a way to get my house cleaned for free."

A blonde wanted to go ice fishing. She'd seen many books on the subject, and finally, after getting all the necessary tools together, she made for the ice. After positioning her comfy footstool, she started to make a circular cut in the ice. Suddenly, from the sky, a voice boomed,

"THERE ARE NO FISH UNDER THE ICE."

Startled, the blonde moved further down the ice, poured a thermos of cappuccino, and began to cut yet another hole. Again from the heavens the voice bellowed,

"THERE ARE NO FISH UNDER THE ICE."

The blonde, now worried, moved away, clear down to the opposite end of the ice. She set up her stool once more and tried again to cut her hole. The voice came once more,

"THERE ARE NO FISH UNDER THE ICE." She stopped, looked skyward, and said, "IS THAT YOU LORD?"

The voice replied, "No, this is the manager of the hockey rink."

A couple goes out to dinner to celebrate their 50th wedding anniversary.

On the way home, she notices a tear in his eye and asks if he's getting sentimental because they're celebrating 50 wonderful years together. He replies, "No, I was thinking about the time before we got married.

Your father threatened me with a shotgun and said he'd have me thrown in jail for 50 years if I didn't marry you. Tomorrow I would've been a free man!"

Two old men have been best friends for years, and they both live to their early 90's, when one of them suddenly falls deathly ill. His friend comes to visit him on his deathbed, and they're reminiscing about their long friendship, when the dying man's friend asks, "Listen, when you die, do me a favor. I want to know if there's baseball in heaven."

The dying man said, "We've been friends for years, this I'll do for you." And then he dies.

A couple days later, his surviving friend is sleeping when he hears his friend's voice. The voice says, "I've got some good news and some bad news. The good news is that there's baseball in heaven."

"What's the bad news?"

"You're pitching on Wednesday."

Two old men are talking about their aches, pains and bodily functions.

One seventy-year-old man says, "I have this problem. I pee like clockwork at 7AM every morning."

The other old man says, "So what's your problem?"

"I don't wake up until nine."

A wise old gentleman retired and purchased a modest home near a junior high school. He spent the first few weeks of his retirement in peace and contentment. Then a new school year began.

The very next afternoon three young boys, full of youthful, after-school enthusiasm, came down his street, beating merrily on every trashcan they encountered. The crashing percussion continued day after day, until finally the wise old man decided it was time to take some action.

The next afternoon, he walked out to meet the young percussionists as they banged their way down the street. Stopping them, he said, "You kids are a lot of fun. I like to see you express your exuberance like that. In fact, I used to do the same thing when I was your age. Will you do me a favor? I'll give you each a dollar if you'll promise to come around every day and do your thing."

The kids were elated and continued to do a bang-up job on the trashcans. After a few days, the old-timer greeted the kids again, but this time he had a sad smile on his face. "This recession's really putting a big dent in my income," he told them. "From now on, I'll only be able to pay you 50 cents to beat on the cans." The noisemakers were obviously displeased, but they accepted his offer and continued their afternoon ruckus. A few days later, the retiree approached them again as they drummed their way down the street.

"Look," he said, "I haven't received my Social Security check yet, so I'm not going to be able to give you more than 25 cents. Will that be okay?" "A lousy quarter?" the drum leader exclaimed. "If you think we're going to waste our time, beating these cans around for a quarter, you're nuts! No way, mister. We quit!" And the old man enjoyed peace.

A 60-year-old man went to a doctor for a check-up. The doctor told him, "You're in terrific shape. There's nothing wrong with you. Why, you might live forever; you have the body of a 35-year-old. By the way, how old was your father when he died?"

The 60-year-old responded, "Did I say he was dead?"

The doctor was surprised and asked, "How old is he and is he very active?"

The 60-year-old responded, "Well, he is 82 years old and he still goes skiing three times a season and surfing three times a week during the summer."

The doctor couldn't believe it. So, he asked, "Well, how old was your grandfather when he died?"

The paitient responded again, "Did I say he was dead?"

The doctor was astonished. He said, "You mean to tell me you are 60 years old and both your father and your grandfather are alive? Is your grandfather very active?"

The 60-year-old said, "He goes skiing at least once a season and surfing once a week during the summer. Not only that," said the patient, "my grandfather is 106 years old, and next week he is getting married again."

The doctor said, "At 106-years, why on earth would your grandfather want to get married?"

His patient looked up at the doctor and said, "Did I say he wanted to?"

"Give me a sentence about a public servant," said the Mother helping her son at home.

The small boy wrote: "The fireman came down the ladder pregnant."

The mother took her son aside to correct him. "Don't you know what pregnant means?" she asked.

"Sure," said the young boy confidently. "It means 'carrying a child.'"

An 80-year-old couple were having problems remembering things, so they decided to go to their doctor to get checked out to make sure nothing was wrong with them. When they arrived at the doctor's, they explained to the doctor about the problems they were having with their memory.

After checking the couple out, the doctor tells them that they were physically okay but might want to start writing things down and make notes to help them remember things. The couple thanked the doctor and left.

Later that night while watching TV, the old man got up from his chair and his wife asks, "Where are you going?"

He replies, "To the kitchen."

She asks, "Will you get me a bowl of ice cream?"

He replies, "Sure."

She then asks him, "Don't you think you should write it down so you can remember it?"

He says, "No, I can remember that."

She then says, "Well, I also would like some strawberries on top. You better write that down cause I know you'll forget."

He says, "I can remember that, you want a bowl of ice cream with strawberries."

She replies, "Well, I also would like whip cream on top. I know you will forget that so you better write it down."

Irritated, he says, "I don't need to write that down, I can remember that." He then fumes into the kitchen.

After about 20 minutes he returns from the kitchen and hands her a plate of bacon and eggs.

She stares at the plate for a moment and says, "You forgot my toast."

Two elderly women were out driving in a large car of which both could barely see over the dashboard. As they were cruising along they came to an intersection. The stoplight was red but they just went on through. The woman in the passenger seat thought to herself

"I must be losing it, I could have sworn we just went through a red light."

After a few more minutes they came to another intersection and the light was red again and again they went right though. This time the woman in the passenger seat was almost sure that the light had been red but was really concerned that she was losing it. She was getting nervous and decided to pay very close attention to the road and the next intersection to see what was going on.

At the next intersection, sure enough, the light was definitely red and they went right through and she turned to the other woman and said, "Mildred! Did you know we just ran through three red lights in a row! You could have killed us!"

Mildred turned to her and said, "Oh, am I driving?"

A rabbi was called to a Miami Beach Nursing Home to perform a wedding.

An anxious old man met him at the door. The rabbi sat down to counsel the old man and asked several questions. "Do you love her?"

The old man replied, "I guess."

"Is she a good Jewish woman?"

"I don't know for sure," the old man answered.

"Does she have lots of money?" asked the rabbi.

"I doubt it."

"Then why are you marrying her?" the rabbi asked.

"She can drive at night," the old man said.

Three ladies were discussing the travails of getting older. One said, "Sometimes I catch myself with a jar of mayonnaise in my hand, while standing in front of the refrigerator, and I can't remember whether I need to put it away, or start making a sandwich."

The second lady chimed in with, "Yes, sometimes I find myself on the landing of the stairs and can't remember whether I was on my way up or on my way down."

The third one responded, "Well, ladies, I'm glad I don't have that problem. Knock on wood," as she rapped her knuckles on the table, and then said, "That must be the door, I'll get it!"

With the average cost for a Nursing Home per day reaching $188.00,there is a better way when we get old & feeble. I have already checked on reservations at the Holiday Inn for a combined long-term stay discount and senior discount of $49.23 per night. That leaves $138.77 a day for:

1. Breakfast, lunch and dinner in any restaurant I want, or room service.

2. Laundry, gratuities and special TV movies. Plus, they provide a swimming pool, a workout room, a lounge, washer, dryer, etc. Most have free toothpaste and razors, and all have free shampoo and soap.

3. They treat you like a customer, not a patient. $5 worth of tips a day will have the entire staff scrambling to help you. There is a city Bus stop out front, and

seniors ride free. The Handicap bus will also pick you up (if you fake a decent limp). To meet other nice people, call a Church bus on Sundays. For a change of scenery, take the Airport shuttle Bus and eat at one of the nice restaurants there. While you're at the airport, fly somewhere. Otherwise, the cash keeps building up.

4. It takes months to get into decent nursing homes. Holiday Inn will take your reservation today. And you are not stuck in one place forever, you can move from Inn to Inn, or even from city to city. Want to see Hawaii? They have a Holiday Inn there too.

5. TV broken? Light bulbs need changing? Need a mattress replaced? No problem. They fix everything, and apologize for the inconvenience. The Inn has a night security person and daily room service. The maid checks to see if

you are ok. If not, they will call the undertaker or an ambulance. If you fall and break a hip, Medicare will pay for the hip, and Holiday Inn will upgrade you to a suite for the rest of your life.

6. And no worries about visits from family. They will always be glad to find you, and probably check in for a few days mini-vacation. The grand kids can use the pool. What more can you ask for?

So: As I reach the Golden age I'm facing it with a grin. I'll just check into the nearest Holiday Inn!

A man plays a game of poker with his friends every weekend. One evening he comes home after his game, and tells his wife to pack her bags, she is going to live with one of his poker buddies.

"What are you talking about?" she asks.

"I lost you to him in poker tonight, just pack your bags!"

"How could you lose me in a poker game," the exasperated woman asks.

"It wasn't easy; I had to fold with four aces."

Three elderly gentlemen were talking about what their grandchildren would be saying about them fifty years from now.

"I would like my grandchildren to say, 'He was successful in business'," declared the first man.

"Fifty years from now," said the second, "I want them to say, 'He was a loyal family man'."

Turning to the third gent, the first gent asked, "So what do you want them to say about you in fifty years?"

"Me?" the third man replied. "I want them all to say, "He certainly looks good for his age'!"

For the first time in many years, an old man traveled from his rural town to the city to attend a movie. After buying his ticket, he stopped at the concession stand to purchase some popcorn.

Handing the attendant $1.50, he couldn't help but comment, "The last time I came to the movies, popcorn was only 15 cents."

"Well, sir," the attendant replied with a grin, "You're really going to enjoy yourself. We have sound now."

Some thoughts from a retired mind

I was thinking about how a status symbol of today is those cell phones that everyone has clipped onto their belt or purse. I can't afford one, so, I'm wearing my garage door opener.

You know, I spent a fortune on deodorant before I realized that people who avoided me just didn't like me.

I was thinking that women should put pictures of missing husbands on beer cans, and men should put pictures of their missing wives up at the mall!

I was thinking about old age and decided that old age is when you still have something on the ball, but you are just too tired to bounce it.

I thought about making a fitness movie, for folks my age, and call it "Pumping Rust."

I have gotten that dreaded furniture disease: That's when your chest is falling into your drawers!

I've come to realize that the secret to a happy life is not looking like Barbie or Ken and suffering through tofu and rice cakes to stay that way! It's eating chocolate, staying chunky and explaining that you're really a perfect size 6, but you keep it covered with fat so it doesn't get scratched!

I know, when people see a cat's litter box, they always say,

"Oh, have you got a cat?" Just once I want to say, "No, it's for Visitors!"

Employment application blanks always ask 'who is to be notified in case of an emergency' I think you should write, "A Good Doctor!"

Why is it that every time I lose weight it finds me again?

Why do they put pictures of criminals up in the Post Office? What are we supposed to do -- write to these men? Why don't they just put their pictures on the postage stamps so the mailmen could look for them while they deliver the mail? Or better yet, arrest them while they are taking their pictures!

Just once, when someone says, "How are you?" (without

really wanting to know), I'd like to say "Well, I can't keep my teeth in, I pee on myself every time I laugh, my hair is falling out, I cannot see where the heck I'm going most of the time, my back hurts and I pass gas every time I sneeze (and feel like sneezing right now)! I'll bet that'd cure 'em from asking again!

The nice thing about being senile is you can hide your own Easter eggs.

A man and his bride are at a resort for their honeymoon. The resort offers horseback riding and they decide to give it a try. They start off down the trail, when a noise startles the bride's horse. It rears, jostling the bride. The groom jumps off his horse, grabs the reins of the horse, gets right into the horse's face, and says, "That's one!"

The couple rides a while longer. A flock of birds, startled by the horses, flies up out of the brush. Again, the bride's horse jumps back, and she bounces around in the saddle. The groom jumps off his horse, calms the bride's horse, look it in the eyes, and says, "That's two!"

Near the end of the ride, a rabbit runs in front of the couple. The bride's horse is spooked, and the bride falls from the saddle. The groom jumps off his horse, makes sure the bride is not injured, and then says to the horse,

"That's three." He pulls out a gun and shoot the horse, killing it.

The appalled bride scream, "You are a sick man. You're a mean spirited and vicious human being! I can't believe that I married someone as heartless as you!"

The groom looks her in the eye and says, "That's one!"

THE NEW "OVER-40" BARBIES

1.) Bifocals Barbie. Comes with her own set of blended-lens fashion frames in six wild colors (half-frames too!), neck chain and large-print editions of Reader's Digest.

2.) Hot Flash Barbie. Press Barbie's bellybutton and watch her face turn beet red while tiny drops of perspiration appear on her forehead! With hand-held fan and tiny tissues.

3.) Facial Hair Barbie. As Barbie's hormone levels shift, see her whiskers grow! Available with teensy tweezers and magnifying mirror.

4.) Cook's Arms Barbie. Hide Barbie's droopy triceps with these new, roomier-sleeved gowns. Good news on the tummy front, too: muumuus are back! Cellulite cream and loofah sponge optional.

5.) Bunion Barbie. Years of disco dancing in stiletto heels have definitely taken their toll on Barbie's dainty arched feet. Soothe her sores with this pumice stone and plasters, then slip on soft terry mules. Colors: pink, rose, blush.

6.) No More Wrinkles Barbie. Erase those pesky crow's-feet and lip lines with a tube of Skin Sparkle-Spackle, from Barbie's own line of exclusive age-blasting cosmetics.

7.) Soccer Mom Barbie. All that experience as a cheerleader is really paying off as Barbie dusts off her old high school megaphone to root for Babs and Ken Jr. With minivan in robin's egg blue or white, and cooler filled with doughnut holes and fruit punch.

8.) Midlife Crisis Barbie. It's time to ditch Ken. Barbie needs a change, and Bruce (her personal trainer) is just what the doctor ordered, along with Prozac. They're hopping in her new red Miata and heading for the Napa Valley to open a B&B. Comes with real tape of "Breaking Up Is Hard to Do."

9.) Single Mother Barbie. There's not much time for primping anymore! Ken's shacked up with the Swedish au pair in the Dream House and Barbie's across town with Babs and Ken Jr. in a fourth-floor walk-up. Barbie's selling off her old gowns and accessories to raise rent money. Complete garage sale kit included.

10.) Recovery Barbie. Too many parties have finally caught up with the ultimate party girl. Now she does 12 steps instead of dance steps! Clean and sober, she's going to meetings religiously. Comes with little copy of The Big Book, and a six-pack of Diet Coke.

SENIORS TEXTING CODES

ATD - At The Doctors

BFF - Best Friend Fell

BTW - Bring the Wheelchair

BYOT - Bring Your Own Teeth

FWIW - Forgot Where I Was

GGPBL - Gotta Go Pacemaker Battery Low

IMHO - Is My Hearing-Aid On

LMDO - Laughing My Dentures Out

OMMR - On My Massage Recliner

ROFLACGU - Rolling On Floor Laughing And Can't Get Up...

What Generation Are You?

Welcome to the generational assessment test. Note your answer to each of the following questions and review your results at the end.

Who is the ideal figure of motherhood?
A - Eleanor Roosevelt
B - Donna Reed
C - Mrs. Brady
D - Lois Griffin

What did you want to be when you grew up?
A - Part of a nuclear family
B - Someone who makes lots of money
C - Living with your parents
D - Living with your parents

Music should be:
A - Melodic and romantic
B - Annoying to your parents
C - Annoying to your parents
D - Annoying to your parents

The scariest moment in film history was:
A - When the mummy rose from his tomb
B - When the Blob chased Steve McQueen
C - When the alien burst from the man's chest
D - Watching any of the Twilight movies

The most inspiring American is:
A - John Wayne
B - John F. Kennedy
C - John F. Kennedy Jr
D - The boys of South Park

I expect my retirement to be:
A - When I can look back on a happy, fulfilling life
B - An opportunity to finally write my novel
C - An agonizing slide into abject poverty
D - A daily struggle to survive in a horribly polluted world

America is becoming:
A - More impersonal
B - More frightening

C - More expensive
D - Whatever

The American Dream is:
A - A house with a two-car garage
B - A healthy family
C - Winning the lottery
D - Touring with Justin Bieber

My college major was:
A - Business
B - Liberal arts
C - Secondary to my bartending job
D - Something far, far away

A good meal would be:
A - Meat and potatoes
B - Vegetarian macrobiotic
C - From a drive-up window
D - Microwaveable

My favorite footwear is:
A - Sensible shoes
B - Earth shoes
C - Converse high-tops
D - Doc Martens

I learned to drive behind the wheel of a:

A - '53 Packard
B - '61 VW
C - '78 Pinto
D - PS3

The "woman":
A - Marilyn Monroe
B - Raquel Welch
C - Julia Roberts
D - Megan Fox

The "man":
A - Cary Grant
B - Paul McCartney
C - Eddie Vedder
D - Ryan Reynolds

Lost idol:
A - James Dean
B - Jim Morrison
C - Kurt Cobain
D - Mario Bros

Fashion accessory best forgotten:
A - Double knit
B - Bell bottoms
C - Skinny ties
D - Ridiculously baggy pants

The best way to spend a weekend is:
A - Playing golf
B - Consciousness raising
C - Mountain biking
D - Internet surfing

I remember where I was when:
A - The Japanese surrendered
B - John F. Kennedy was shot
C - John Lennon was shot
D - Brad and Angelina got engaged

Life changing movie:
A - East of Eden
B - Easy Rider
C - Heathers
D - Anchor Man

Life-changing novel:
A - Catcher in the Rye
B - Fear and Loathing in Las Vegas
C - Bright Lights Big City
D - Vampire Diaries

Sports hero:
A - Mickey Mantle
B - O.J. Simpson

C - Michael Jordan
D - Tebow

Celebrity my generation would rather not claim:
A - Joe McCarthy
B - Barry Manilow
C - Vanilla Ice
D - Hannah Montana

Computers are:
A - Frightening and disconcerting
B - Complicated
C - Part of life
D - My only link to the outside world

The father is the one who:
A - Brings home the bacon
B - Is attuned to his sensitive side
C - Left years ago
D - Holds the remote control

My after-college plans:
A - Work hard to help build a strong America
B - Take my pick of many job opportunities

C - Take my pick of many low-paying temp services
D - Would you like fries with that?

My generation's most annoying fad is:
A - Nuclear testing
B - Hula hoops
C - Body piercing
D - Unemployment

The voice of my generation:
A - Walter Cronkite
B - Bob Dylan
C - Madonna
D - Kim Kardashian

My generation's biggest fear is:
A - Heart disease
B - Getting older
C - Collection agencies
D - Not getting likes on Facebook

RESULTS:

If you answer mostly A, you're a pre-boomer. If you answer mostly B, you're a Baby-Boomer. If you answer mostly C, you're in Generation X. If you answer mostly D, you're in Generation Y.

Aging Is When...

1. Everything hurts and what doesn't hurt, doesn't work.

2. The gleam in your eye is the sun hitting your bifocals.

3. You feel like the night after, but you haven't been anywhere.

4. Your little black book contains only names ending in M.D.

5. You get winded playing chess.

6. Your children begin to look middle-aged.

7. You finally reach the top of the ladder and find it leaning.

8. You join a health club, but don't go.

9. You begin to outlive enthusiasm.

10. Your mind makes contracts that your body can't keep.

11. You look forward to a dull evening.

12. "25 Years Ago Today", is your favorite part of the newspaper.

13. You sit in a rocking chair and can't get it going.

14. Your knees buckle and your belt won't.

15. The best part of the day is over when the alarm clock goes off.

16. Your back goes out more often than you do.

17. You sink your teeth into a steak and they stay there.

18. You forget, why you are reading this.

A man is enjoying a late night drink when he notices that a man who must have had too much to drink has fallen from his stool. He runs over and puts him back on the stool, only to watch him fall again a few minutes later.

He feels sorry for the man and calls a cab after getting the man's address from his driver's license. The man has a terrible time making it to the cab, falling down three more times. The Good Samaritan decides it would be best to ride with the man to insure his safe arrival home.

The man stumbles and falls two more times from the cab to the front door.

Hearing a commotion, the man's wife opens the front door.

"Ma'am, I brought your husband home," the Samaritan exclaims.

"Thank you so much, but where's his wheelchair?" asks the wife.

Driving through a small town, a man comes to an intersection where the cross traffic has the right of way. Instead of coming to a full stop, he slows, notices a break in traffic and makes a right turn. No sooner had he turned than a cop puts on his lights and pulls the man over.

"You didn't stop at that intersection," says the cop.

"I know officer, but I did slow down," replies the man.

"Yes, but you didn't stop."

"No, but I slowed down."

"But you didn't stop," the cop angrily replies.

"No, but what is the difference really?" asks the young man.

The cop takes out his nightstick and starts to hit the young man. "Now, what do you want me to do," he asks, "slow down or stop?"

Submitted from a fan:

Today at the drugstore, the clerk was a gent.

From my purchase this chap took off ten percent.

I asked for the cause of a lesser amount;

And he answered, "Because of the Seniors Discount."

I went to McDonald's for a burger and fries;

And there, once again, got quite a surprise.

The clerk poured some coffee, which he handed to me.

He said, "For you, Seniors, the coffee is free."

Understand---I'm not old---I'm merely mature;

But some things are changing, temporarily, I'm sure.

The newspaper print gets smaller each day,

And people speak softer---can't hear what they say.

My teeth are my own (I have the receipt.),

and my glasses identify people I meet.

Oh, I've slowed down a bit... not a lot, I am sure.

You see, I'm not old... I'm only mature.

The gold in my hair has been bleached by the sun.

You should see all the damage that chlorine has done.

Washing my hair has turned it all white,

But don't call it gray... saying "blond" is just right.

My car is all paid for... not a nickel is owed.

Yet a kid yells, "Old duffer... get off of the road!"

My car has no scratches... not even a dent.

Still I get all that guff from a punk who's "Hell bent."

My friends all get older... much faster than me.

They seem much more wrinkled, from what I can see.

I've got "character lines," not wrinkles... for sure,

But don't call me old... just call me mature.

The steps in the houses they're building today

Are so high that they take... your breath all away;

And the streets are much steeper than ten years ago.

That should explain why my walking is slow.

But I'm keeping up on what's hip and what's new,

And I think I can still dance a mean boogaloo.

I'm still in the running... in this I'm secure,

I'm not really old... I'm only mature.

Contact Information:

Share your own personal stories and jokes with Christopher at funnyhypermagicboy.com or by emailing christopherjamescomedy@gmail.com.

Join the Facebook Fan Club: Search for Funny Hyper Magic Boy or go to www.facebook.com/funnyhypermagicboy.

Over 200 Youtube videos online. Visit funnyhypermagicboy.com for the latest links and updates.

Made in the USA
San Bernardino, CA
28 April 2014